THE TRAIN OF STATES

Peter Sís

GREENWILLOW BOOKS
An Imprint of HarperCollinsPublishers

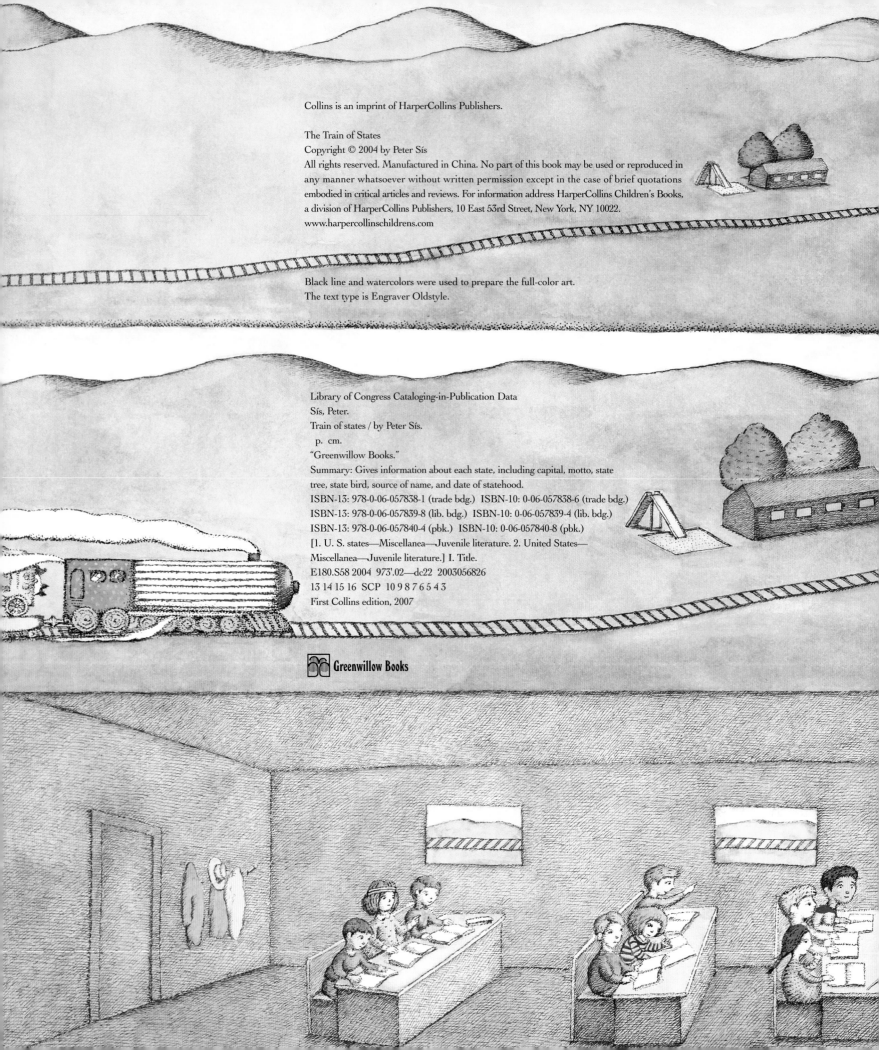

Library of Congress Cataloging-in-Publication Data
Sís, Peter.
Train of states / by Peter Sís.
    p. cm.
"Greenwillow Books."
Summary: Gives information about each state, including capital, motto, state tree, state bird, source of name, and date of statehood.
ISBN-13: 978-0-06-057838-1 (trade bdg.) ISBN-10: 0-06-057838-6 (trade bdg.)
ISBN-13: 978-0-06-057839-8 (lib. bdg.) ISBN-10: 0-06-057839-4 (lib. bdg.)
ISBN-13: 978-0-06-057840-4 (pbk.) ISBN-10: 0-06-057840-8 (pbk.)
[1. U. S. states—Miscellanea—Juvenile literature. 2. United States—Miscellanea—Juvenile literature.] I. Title.
E180.S58 2004 973'.02—dc22 2003056826
13 14 15 16 SCP 10 9 8 7 6 5 4 3
First Collins edition, 2007

Greenwillow Books

*To twenty-two years in the United States
and twenty years with Greenwillow Books*

The Train of States is a personal journey that combines my love for my adopted country with my admiration for antique circus wagons. There are hundreds of facts, symbols, moments from history, tidbits, and details presented on these pages—many of them open to interpretation; several of them the topic of ongoing debate. I hope my book will lead you on your own journeys of discovery.

Very special thanks to Martha Mihalick and Anne Dunn, fact-checkers extraordinaire, and to Virginia Bartow of the Humanities and Social Sciences Library, The New York Public Library, for their relentless investigation of the materials presented in this book.

—PETER SÍS

"LIBERTY AND INDEPENDENCE"

PEACH
BLOSSOM

AMERICAN
HOLLY

SWEET
GOLDENROD

LADYBUG

WEAKFISH

TIGER
SWALLOWTAIL

BLUE HEN CHICKEN

FIRST STATE

1. DELAWARE DATE OF STATEHOOD December 7, 1787

Named for Baron de la Warr, English governor of Virginia

 Dover

American holly

 peach blossom

blue hen chicken

In 1880, the first beauty contest in the U.S. was held in Rehoboth Beach. Thomas Edison was one of the three judges.

BENJAMIN FRANKLIN

HEMLOCK

HERSHEY'S KISS

RUFFED GROUSE

TRILOBITE

MOUNTAIN LAUREL

GREAT DANE

KEYSTONE STATE

BROOK TROUT

BETSY ROSS

MARIAN ANDERSON

FIRST LIBRARY

JAMES BUCHANAN

"VIRTUE, LIBERTY, AND INDEPENDENCE"

2. PENNSYLVANIA December 12, 1787

Named for Adm. Sir William Penn and the Latin *silva*, meaning "woodland"

 Harrisburg

 hemlock

 mountain laurel

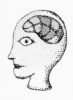 ruffed grouse

 When legislators made the Great Dane the state dog in 1965, they voted with yips, growls, and barks.

GARDEN STATE

"LIBERTY AND PROSPERITY"

3. NEW JERSEY December 18, 1787

DATE OF STATEHOOD

Named for the Channel Isle of Jersey in England

 Trenton

 red oak

 violet

 eastern goldfinch

 The "Bone Wars"—a bitter feud between paleontologists—began in New Jersey ten years after the first nearly complete dinosaur skeleton was found there in 1858.

SHARK TOOTH

CHEROKEE ROSE

PEACH STATE

JIMMY CARTER

BROWN THRASHER

TIGER SWALLOWTAIL

LARGEMOUTH BASS

LIVE OAK

RIGHT WHALE

"WISDOM, JUSTICE, AND MODERATION"

DATE OF STATEHOOD

4. GEORGIA January 2, 1788

Named for England's King George II

 Atlanta

 live oak

 Cherokee rose

 brown thrasher

Civil rights activist and Atlanta native Martin Luther King, Jr., was born Michael Luther King; he was renamed when he was six.

CONSTITUTION STATE

AMERICAN ROBIN

MOUNTAIN LAUREL

YANKEE DOODLE

GEORGE W. BUSH

P. T. BARNUM

WHITE OAK

OYSTERS

"HE WHO TRANSPLANTED STILL SUSTAINS"

DATE OF STATEHOOD

5. CONNECTICUT January 9, 1788

Named for the Mohegan Indian *quinnehtukqut*, meaning "beside the long tidal river."

 Hartford

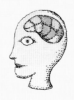 white oak

 The first hamburger was served in 1895 at Louie's Lunch in New Haven.

 mountain laurel

 American robin

MASSASOIT

TURKEY

BLACK-CAPPED CHICKADEE

JOHN ADAMS

JOHN QUINCY ADAMS

PHILLIS WHEATLEY

BAY STATE

LOUISA MAY ALCOTT

JOHN F. KENNEDY

GEORGE H. W. BUSH

PAUL REVERE

AMERICAN ELM

MAYFLOWER

NEPTUNE SHELL

NORTHERN RIGHT WHALE

LADYBUG

ALEXANDER GRAHAM BELL

CAPE COD

COD

BOSTON TERRIER

"BY THE SWORD WE SEEK PEACE,
BUT PEACE ONLY UNDER LIBERTY"

MORGAN HORSE

Named for the Algonquian Indian word meaning "at the big hill"

 Boston

 American elm

 mayflower

 black-capped chickadee

In 1891, James Naismith invented the game of basketball in Springfield. The first game was played with a soccer ball and peach baskets hung ten feet in the air.

FIRST REFRIGERATOR

BALTIMORE CHECKERSPOT

HARRIET TUBMAN

KING WILLIAM'S SCHOOL

STRIPED BASS

WHITE OAK

DIAMONDBACK TERRAPIN

BLACK-EYED SUSAN

BALTIMORE ORIOLE

OLD LINE STATE

CALICO CAT

CHESAPEAKE BAY RETRIEVER

"MANLY DEEDS, WOMANLY WORDS"

DATE OF STATEHOOD

7. MARYLAND April 28, 1788

Named for Henrietta Maria, queen to England's Charles I

 Annapolis

 white oak

 black-eyed Susan

 Baltimore oriole

 Francis Scott Key wrote "The Star-Spangled Banner" from a British ship in the Baltimore harbor in 1814.

PALMETTO STATE

ANDREW JACKSON

BLUE GRANITE

YELLOW JESSAMINE

SPOTTED SALAMANDER

PEACH

CAROLINA WREN

EASTERN TIGER SWALLOWTAIL

"PREPARED IN MIND AND RESOURCES"
"WHILE I BREATHE, I HOPE"

BOYKIN SPANIEL

DATE OF STATEHOOD

May 23, 1788

Named for England's King Charles I

 Columbia

 palmetto

 yellow jessamine

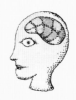 Carolina wren

 South Carolina is considered to have some of the most pristine nesting areas for loggerhead sea turtles, a threatened species.

BERYL

CORNISH-WINDSOR BRIDGE

GRANITE

GRANITE STATE

FRANKLIN PIERCE

PURPLE LILAC

PINK LADY'S SLIPPER

FIRST FREE LIBRARY

PURPLE FINCH

WHITE BIRCH

"LIVE FREE OR DIE"

STRIPED BASS

KARNER BLUE

BROOK TROUT

9. NEW HAMPSHIRE

DATE OF STATEHOOD

June 21, 1788

Named for Hampshire County, England

Concord

white birch

purple lilac

purple finch

The Brattle Organ in Portsmouth's St. John's Church is the oldest pipe organ in the United States. Still played on special occasions, it dates back to 1708.

GEORGE WASHINGTON | THOMAS JEFFERSON | JAMES MADISON | JAMES MONROE | WILLIAM HENRY HARRISON | JOHN TYLER | ZACHARY TAYLOR | WOODROW WILSON

CARDINAL

BROOK TROUT

"THUS ALWAYS TO TYRANTS"

MOUNT VERNON

MONTICELLO

TIGER SWALLOWTAIL

DOGWOOD

POCAHONTAS

OLD DOMINION STATE

10. VIRGINIA June 25, 1788

DATE OF STATEHOOD

Named for England's Queen Elizabeth I, the Virgin Queen

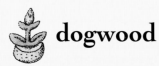 Richmond

 dogwood

 dogwood

 cardinal

 Both the Revolutionary War and the Civil War ended in Virginia, the first in Yorktown in 1781 and the second at Appomattox Court House in 1865.

EMPIRE STATE

ROSE
BLUEBIRD
BROOK TROUT
PRETZEL
SUGAR MAPLE

FRANKLIN D. ROOSEVELT
THEODORE ROOSEVELT
SUSAN B. ANTHONY
MARTIN VAN BUREN
MILLARD FILLMORE
SOJOURNER TRUTH
ELEANOR ROOSEVELT

"EVER UPWARD"

11. NEW YORK
DATE OF STATEHOOD
July 26, 1788
Named for England's Duke of York

 Albany

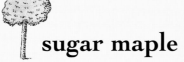
 sugar maple

rose

bluebird

 Chittenango, birthplace of *The Wizard of Oz* author L. Frank Baum, has a yellow brick road and an annual Munchkin parade.

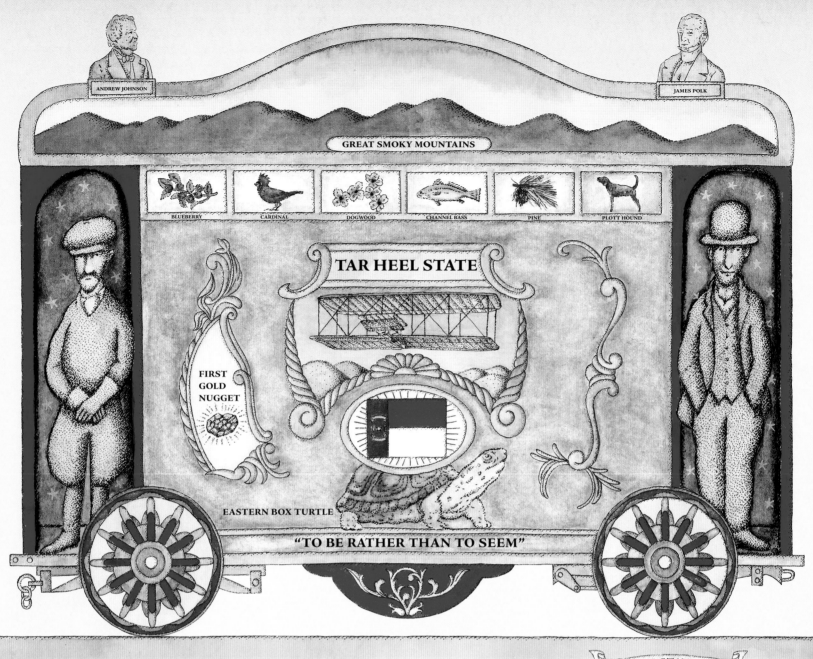

ANDREW JOHNSON

JAMES POLK

GREAT SMOKY MOUNTAINS

BLUEBERRY CARDINAL DOGWOOD CHANNEL BASS PINE PLOTT HOUND

TAR HEEL STATE

FIRST GOLD NUGGET

EASTERN BOX TURTLE

"TO BE RATHER THAN TO SEEM"

DATE OF STATEHOOD

12. NORTH CAROLINA
November 21, 1789

Named for England's King Charles I

 Raleigh

 pine

 dogwood

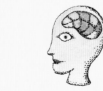 cardinal

The Roanoke Island colony vanished between 1587, when leader John White went back to England for supplies, and 1590, when he returned. The only clue was the word "Croatoan" carved into a tree.

RED MAPLE

GREENING APPLE

RHODE ISLAND RED

VIOLET

STRIPED BASS

OCEAN STATE

OLDEST SCHOOLHOUSE

OLDEST CAROUSEL

FIRST CIRCUS

"HOPE"

DATE OF STATEHOOD

13. RHODE ISLAND May 29, 1790

Named for the Greek island of Rhodes

 Providence

 red maple

The Flying Horse Carousel in Watch Hill is the oldest carousel in the U.S. in continuous operation.

 **violet**

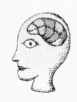 **Rhode Island red**

CHESTER ARTHUR

CALVIN COOLIDGE

"FREEDOM AND UNITY"

WALLEYE PIKE

BROOK TROUT

HERMIT THRUSH

MONARCH

HONEYBEE

SUGAR MAPLE

RED CLOVER

NORTHERN LEOPARD FROG

MAPLE SYRUP

MORGAN HORSE

GREEN MOUNTAIN STATE

DATE OF STATEHOOD

14. VERMONT March 4, 1791

Named for the French words *vert mont*, meaning "green mountain"

  Montpelier

sugar maple

Vermont's was the first state constitution to outlaw slavery—in 1777.

 red clover

 hermit thrush

BLUEGRASS MUSIC

BLUEGRASS STATE

ABRAHAM LINCOLN

CARDINAL

KENTUCKY BASS

VICEROY

MAMMOTH CAVE

BEAGLE

GOLDENROD

GRAY SQUIRREL

TULIP TREE

"UNITED WE STAND, DIVIDED WE FALL"

DATE OF STATEHOOD

15. KENTUCKY
June 1, 1792

Named for the Iroquois Indian word meaning "land of tomorrow"

 Frankfort

 tulip tree

 goldenrod

 cardinal

More than six billion dollars' worth of gold is held in the underground vaults of Fort Knox. This is the largest amount of gold stored anywhere in the world.

ELVIS PRESLEY

MOCKINGBIRD

ZEBRA SWALLOWTAIL

FIRST U.S. GUIDE DOG

CHANNEL CATFISH

VOLUNTEER STATE

LARGEMOUTH BASS

BOX TURTLE

LIGHTNING BUG

TULIP TREE

IRIS

RACCOON

"AGRICULTURE AND COMMERCE"

16. TENNESSEE June 1, 1796

DATE OF STATEHOOD

Named for *Tanasi,* an important Cherokee Indian village

 Nashville

 tulip tree

 iris

 mockingbird

 Morris Frank from Nashville was the first American to use a guide dog for the blind. His dog, Buddy, was a female German shepherd he brought home from a guide dog school in Switzerland.

BUCKEYE STATE

RUTHERFORD B. HAYES
JAMES GARFIELD
ULYSSES S. GRANT
BENJAMIN HARRISON
WILLIAM McKINLEY
WILLIAM H. TAFT
WARREN HARDING

CARDINAL

FIRST CHEWING GUM PATENT

FIRST HOT DOG

NEIL ARMSTRONG

TECUMSEH

ANNIE OAKLEY

SCARLET CARNATION

JOHN GLENN

BLACK RACER

TRILOBITE

FIRST PROFESSIONAL BASEBALL TEAM

BUCKEYE

"WITH GOD ALL THINGS ARE POSSIBLE"

DATE OF STATEHOOD

17. OHIO March 1, 1803

Named for the Iroquois Indian word *oheo*, meaning "great river"

 Columbus

 buckeye

 In 1879, Cleveland became the first city in the U.S. to have electric street lamps.

 scarlet carnation

 cardinal

PELICAN STATE

BALD CYPRESS · CATAHOULA LEOPARD DOG · MAGNOLIA · IRIS · BLACK BEAR · ACCORDION

NEW ORLEANS

BROWN PELICAN

ALLIGATOR

"UNION, JUSTICE, AND CONFIDENCE"

18. LOUISIANA April 30, 1812

DATE OF STATEHOOD

Named for King Louis XIV of France

 Baton Rouge

 bald cypress

 magnolia

 brown pelican

 The town of Jean Lafitte is named after the legendary buccaneer and veteran of the Battle of New Orleans and War of 1812.

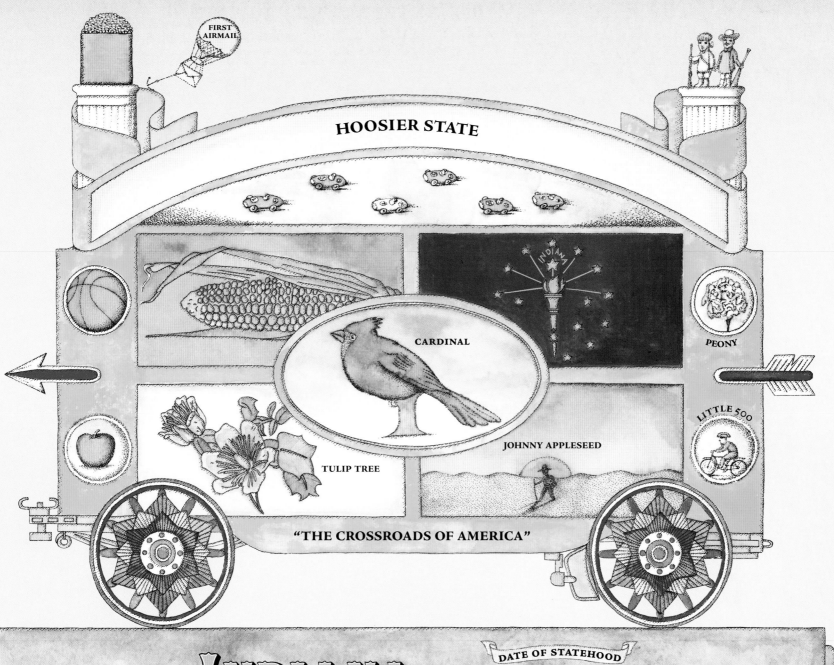

HOOSIER STATE

FIRST AIRMAIL

CARDINAL

INDIANA

PEONY

TULIP TREE

JOHNNY APPLESEED

LITTLE 500

"THE CROSSROADS OF AMERICA"

DATE OF STATEHOOD

19. INDIANA December 11, 1816

Name created by settlers, meaning "land of the Indians"

 Indianapolis

tulip tree

 peony

 cardinal

So many slaves were sheltered in Levi Coffin's Fountain City home that it was known as the "Grand Central Station" of the Underground Railroad.

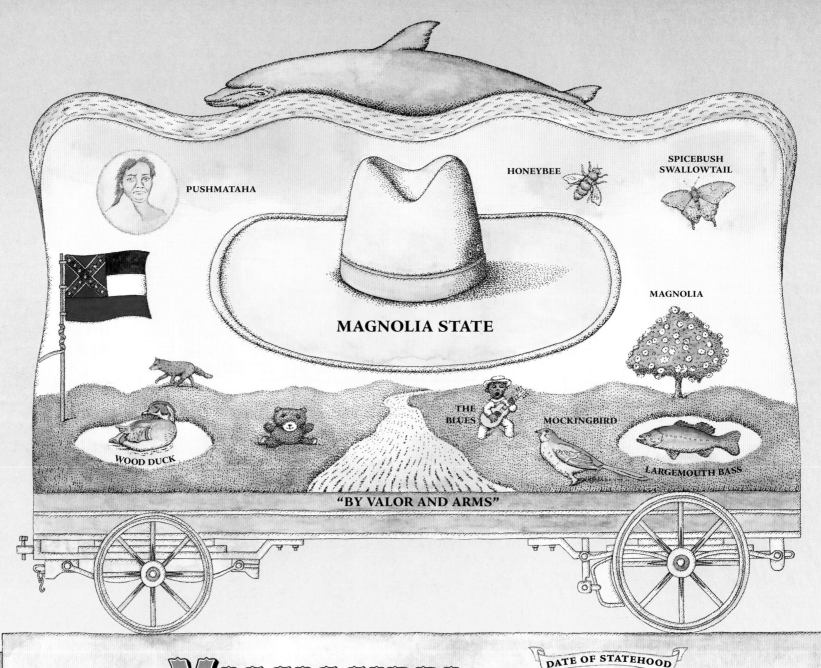

PUSHMATAHA

HONEYBEE

SPICEBUSH SWALLOWTAIL

MAGNOLIA STATE

MAGNOLIA

THE BLUES

MOCKINGBIRD

WOOD DUCK

LARGEMOUTH BASS

"BY VALOR AND ARMS"

DATE OF STATEHOOD

20. MISSISSIPPI December 10, 1817

Named for the Chippewa Indian words *mici zibi*, meaning "great river"

 Jackson

 magnolia

 magnolia

 mockingbird

 On May 11, 1887, a 6 x 8 inch gopher turtle completely encased in ice fell from the sky during a severe hailstorm near Bovina.

PRAIRIE STATE

"STATE SOVEREIGNTY, NATIONAL UNION"

RONALD REAGAN

ILLINOIS

MONARCH

WHITE OAK

BLUEGILL

CARDINAL

WHITE-TAILED DEER

VIOLET

ABRAHAM LINCOLN

CHICAGO

21. ILLINOIS December 3, 1818

Named for a French corruption of the Algonquian Indian word meaning "superior men"

 Springfield

 white oak

 violet

 cardinal

 The Home Insurance Building in Chicago was the world's first modern skyscraper. It was 138 feet high.

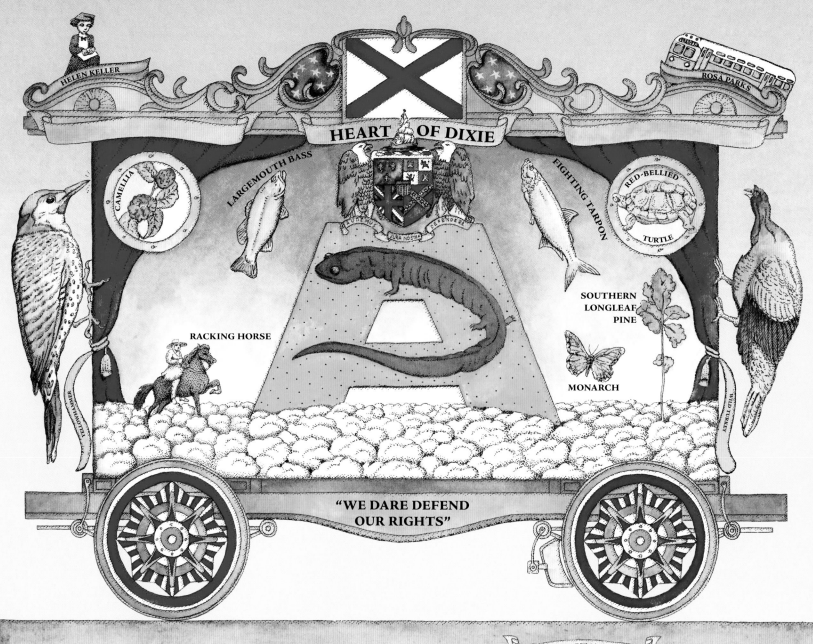

HELEN KELLER

ROSA PARKS

HEART OF DIXIE

CAMELLIA

LARGEMOUTH BASS

FIGHTING TARPON

RED-BELLIED TURTLE

RACKING HORSE

YELLOWHAMMER

SOUTHERN LONGLEAF PINE

MONARCH

WILD TURKEY

"WE DARE DEFEND OUR RIGHTS"

22. ALABAMA December 14, 1819

DATE OF STATEHOOD

Name may be from the Alibamu Indians, members of the Creek Confederacy.
Possibly from the Choctaw language, *alba ayamule*, meaning "I clear the thicket."

 Montgomery

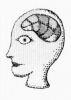 southern longleaf pine

 Rosa Parks refused to give up her seat on a city bus in 1955, which began the Montgomery bus boycott.

 camellia   yellowhammer

PINE TREE STATE

HONEYBEE

CHICKADEE

WINTERGREEN

MAINE COON CAT

WHITE PINE CONE & TASSEL

WILD BLUEBERRY

LANDLOCKED SALMON

"I LEAD"

DATE OF STATEHOOD

23. MAINE March 15, 1820

Name may have originated from explorers referring to the "mainland," from a province in northwestern France, or from a town on the coast of England

 Augusta

 white pine

 white pine cone and tassel

 chickadee

 Margaret Chase Smith of Skowhegan became the first woman to serve in both houses of Congress when she was elected to the Senate in 1948.

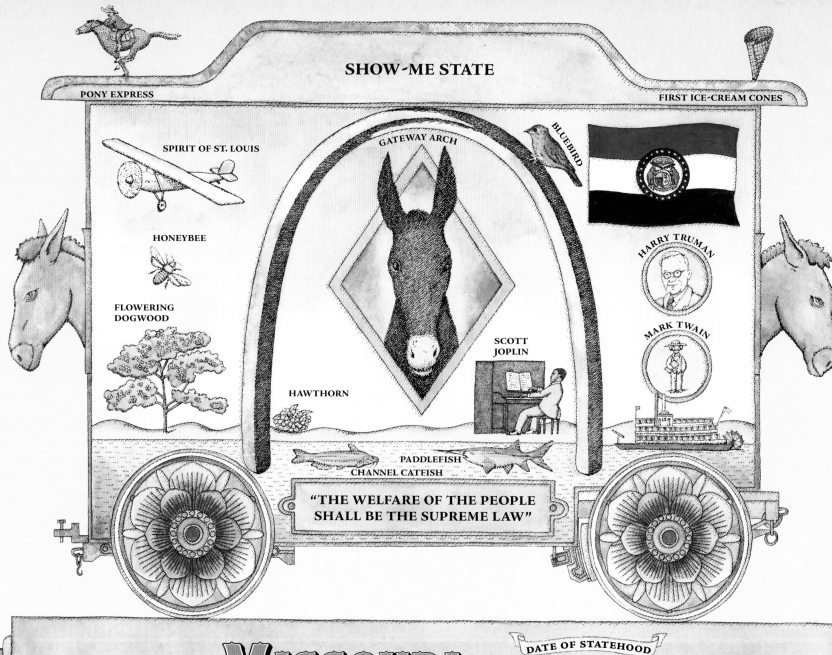

SHOW-ME STATE

PONY EXPRESS

FIRST ICE-CREAM CONES

SPIRIT OF ST. LOUIS

GATEWAY ARCH

BLUEBIRD

HONEYBEE

HARRY TRUMAN

FLOWERING DOGWOOD

MARK TWAIN

SCOTT JOPLIN

HAWTHORN

PADDLEFISH
CHANNEL CATFISH

"THE WELFARE OF THE PEOPLE SHALL BE THE SUPREME LAW"

DATE OF STATEHOOD

24. MISSOURI August 10, 1821

Named for a Sioux Indian tribe; the word *missouri* means "town of the large canoes"

 Jefferson City  flowering dogwood

 hawthorn   bluebird

Ice-cream cones were first served at the Louisiana Purchase Exposition of 1904, also known as the St. Louis World's Fair.

NATURAL STATE

MOCKINGBIRD

WILLIAM J. CLINTON

APPLE BLOSSOM

SOUTH ARKANSAS VINE

RIPE PINK TOMATO

HONEYBEE

PINE

WHITE-TAILED DEER

"THE PEOPLE RULE"

DATE OF STATEHOOD

25. ARKANSAS June 15, 1836

Named for the Quapaw Indians, who were called Akansea, meaning "south wind," by other tribes

 Little Rock

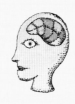 **pine**

The World's Championship Duck Calling Contest is held annually in Stuttgart.

 apple blossom

 **mockingbird**

GREAT LAKE STATE

ANTOINE DE LA MOTHE CADILLAC

"IF YOU SEEK A PLEASANT PENINSULA, LOOK ABOUT YOU"

APPLE BLOSSOM

WHITE PINE

ROBIN

BROOK TROUT

DWARF LAKE IRIS

WHITE-TAILED DEER

PAINTED TURTLE

DATE OF STATEHOOD

26. MICHIGAN January 26, 1837

Named for the Algonquian Indian word *michigama*, meaning "great lake"

 Lansing

 apple blossom

 white pine

 robin

 In 1866 James Vernor of Detroit created his recipe for ginger ale, the first soft drink made in the U.S.

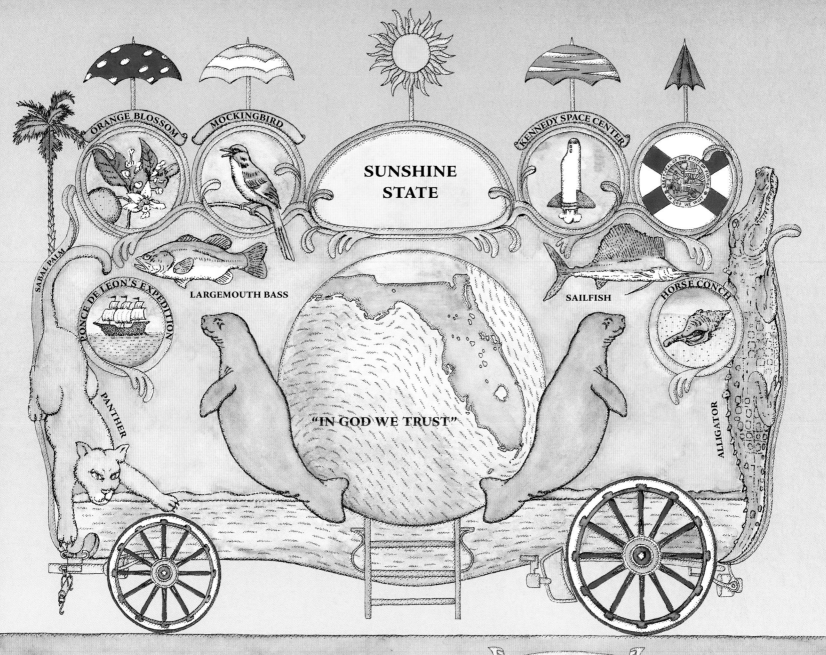

ORANGE BLOSSOM

MOCKINGBIRD

SUNSHINE STATE

KENNEDY SPACE CENTER

SABAL PALM

LARGEMOUTH BASS

PONCE DE LEON'S EXPEDITION

SAILFISH

HORSE CONCH

PANTHER

"IN GOD WE TRUST"

ALLIGATOR

DATE OF STATEHOOD

27. FLORIDA March 3, 1845

Named for Pascua Florida, the Spanish Eastertime "Feast of Flowers," by the explorer Ponce de Leon

 Tallahassee

 sabal palm

 About one million alligators live in the state of Florida.

 orange blossom

 mockingbird

LONE STAR STATE

PRICKLY PEAR CACTUS

BLUEBONNET

MOCKINGBIRD

PECAN

ARMADILLO

DWIGHT D. EISENHOWER

HORNED LIZARD

LYNDON B. JOHNSON

GUADALUPE BASS

MONARCH

MEXICAN FREE-TAILED BAT

LIGHTNING WHELK

"FRIENDSHIP"

DATE OF STATEHOOD

28. TEXAS December 29, 1845

Named for the Caddo Indian word *tejas*, meaning "friends" or "allies"

 **Austin**

 pecan

 **bluebonnet**

 mockingbird

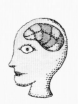 In 1856, Jefferson Davis had camels imported to transport military provisions across west Texas. The Camel Corps had mixed success and ended in 1861.

"OUR LIBERTIES WE PRIZE, AND OUR RIGHTS WE WILL MAINTAIN"

HERBERT HOOVER

GEODE

EASTERN GOLDFINCH

IOWA

HAWKEYE STATE

OAK

WILD ROSE

ANTONÍN DVOŘÁK

29. IOWA December 28, 1846

DATE OF STATEHOOD

Named for the Iowa Indians

 Des Moines

 oak

 wild rose

 eastern goldfinch

 Every year since 1960, the Iowa State Fair has featured a 600-pound butter sculpture of a dairy cow.

BADGER STATE

WISCONSIN
1848

HARRY HOUDINI
FRANK LLOYD WRIGHT
AMERICAN WATER SPANIEL
GENERAL MACARTHUR

TRILOBITE
GREEN BAY PACKERS
ROBIN

DAIRY COW

HONEYBEE
SUGAR MAPLE
WOOD VIOLET
MUSKELLUNGE

"FORWARD"

30. WISCONSIN

DATE OF STATEHOOD

May 29, 1848

Named for the French version of a Chippewa Indian term meaning "grassy place"

 Madison

 **sugar maple**

 **wood violet**

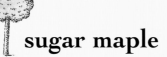 **robin**

 Every year the Great Circus Parade—a re-creation of the old-time street parades of wagons, animals, and performers—rolls through downtown Milwaukee.

JOAQUÍN MURIETA

GOLD GOLDEN TROUT CÉSAR CHÁVEZ

CALIFORNIA QUAIL GARIBALDI

GOLDEN POPPY GOLDEN STATE GRAY WHALE

DOGFACE

MOUNT WHITNEY DESERT TORTOISE

CALIFORNIA REDWOOD RICHARD M. NIXON

MARTHA GRAHAM

"EUREKA"

CALIFORNIA REPUBLIC

DATE OF STATEHOOD

31. CALIFORNIA September 9, 1850

Named for an island paradise in a popular Spanish novel from around 1510

 Sacramento

California redwood

 golden poppy

 California quail

 The first blue jeans were created in 1853 by Levi Strauss and became the uniform for gold prospectors.

PINK AND WHITE LADY'S SLIPPER

RED PINE

NORTH STAR STATE

MOREL

MONARCH

WALLEYE

TWIN CITIES

COMMON LOON

"THE STAR OF THE NORTH"

DATE OF STATEHOOD

32. MINNESOTA May 11, 1858

Named for the Dakota Indian word meaning "sky-tinted water"

 St. Paul

 red pine

pink and white lady's slipper

 common loon

The 130-feet-tall ice palace constructed for the 1888 St. Paul Winter Carnival was by far the city's tallest building at the time.

BEAVER STATE

"SHE FLIES WITH HER OWN WINGS"

WESTERN MEADOWLARK

OREGON GRAPE

DOUGLAS FIR

OREGON SWALLOWTAIL

HAZELNUT

CHINOOK SALMON

CHIEF JOSEPH

PACIFIC GOLDEN CHANTERELLE

STATE OF OREGON
1855

DATE OF STATEHOOD

33. OREGON February 14, 1859

The origins of "Oregon" are uncertain, but it was likely derived from an Indian word.

 Salem

 Douglas fir

 Oregon grape

 western meadowlark

 Formed more than 7,000 years ago, Crater Lake is the deepest lake in the U.S., with an average depth of 1,500 feet and a maximum depth of 1,949 feet.

"TO THE STARS THROUGH DIFFICULTIES"

WESTERN MEADOWLARK

ORNATE BOX TURTLE

COTTONWOOD

NATIVE SUNFLOWER

BARRED TIGER SALAMANDER

CHANNEL CATFISH

HONEYBEE

KANSAS

SUNFLOWER STATE

34. KANSAS January 29, 1861

DATE OF STATEHOOD

Named for the Kansa Indians; *kansa* means "people of the south wind"

 Topeka

cottonwood

 native sunflower

western meadowlark

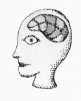 The geographic center of the continental 48 United States is located in Smith County, near Lebanon, in north-central Kansas.

GOLDEN DELICIOUS APPLE

MOUNTAIN STATE

THOMAS "STONEWALL" JACKSON

BROOK TROUT

CARDINAL

MONARCH

SUGAR MAPLE

HONEYBEE

RHODODENDRON

ORGAN CAVE

"MOUNTAINEERS ARE ALWAYS FREE"

35. WEST VIRGINIA June 20, 1863

DATE OF STATEHOOD

Named for England's Queen Elizabeth I, the Virgin Queen

 Charleston

 sugar maple

 The continent's largest conical burial mound is in Moundsville. It is 69 feet high and 295 feet in diameter.

 rhododendron

 cardinal

SILVER STATE

MOUNTAIN BLUEBIRD

LAHONTAN CUTTHROAT TROUT

DESERT TORTOISE

DESERT BIGHORN SHEEP

SAGEBRUSH

TURQUOISE

SINGLE-LEAF PIÑON

BRISTLECONE PINE

"ALL FOR OUR COUNTRY"

DATE OF STATEHOOD

36. NEVADA October 31, 1864

Named for the Spanish word *nevada*, meaning "snow-capped"

 Carson City

 single-leaf piñon and bristlecone pine

 sagebrush

 mountain bluebird

Hard hats were first invented in 1933 specifically for workers on the Hoover Dam, the largest single public works project of its day.

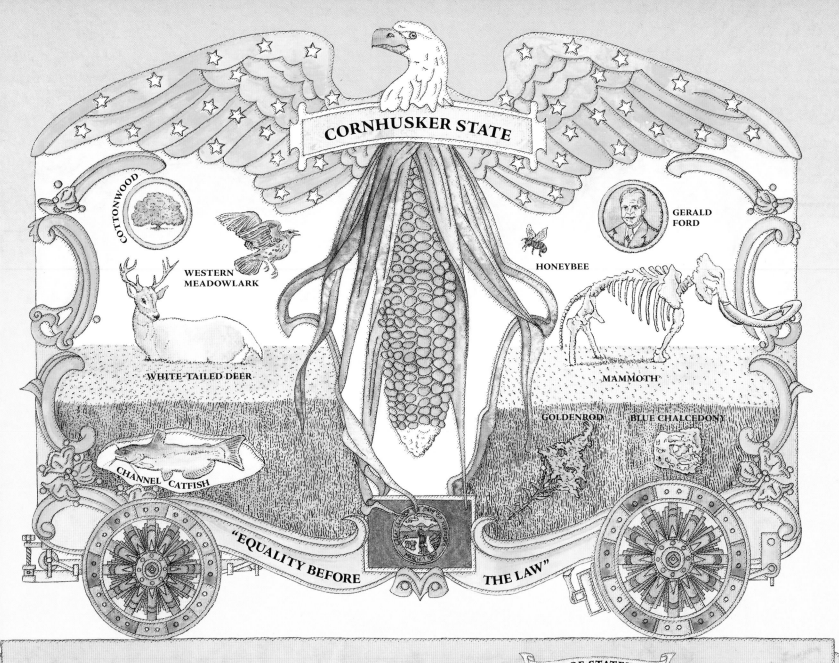

CORNHUSKER STATE

COTTONWOOD

WESTERN MEADOWLARK

WHITE-TAILED DEER

GERALD FORD

HONEYBEE

MAMMOTH

GOLDENROD   BLUE CHALCEDONY

CHANNEL CATFISH

"EQUALITY BEFORE   THE LAW"

37. NEBRASKA March 1, 1867

DATE OF STATEHOOD

Named for the Oto Indian word *nebrathka*, meaning "flat water"

 Lincoln

 cottonwood

 goldenrod

 western meadowlark

 The longest porch swing in the world is in Hebron. It can seat eighteen adults or twenty-four children.

CENTENNIAL STATE "NOTHING WITHOUT THE DEITY"

BLUE GRAMA GRASS BLUE SPRUCE WHITE AND LAVENDER COLUMBINE HAIRSTREAK

GREENBACK CUTTHROAT TROUT LARK BUNTING

38. COLORADO August 1, 1876

DATE OF STATEHOOD

Named for the Spanish word *colorado*, meaning "red" or "ruddy"

 Denver

 blue spruce

 white and lavender columbine

 lark bunting

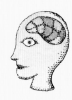 After gold was discovered near Pikes Peak in 1858, the slogan "Pikes Peak or Bust" began appearing painted on prairie schooners (the covered wagons used by pioneers).

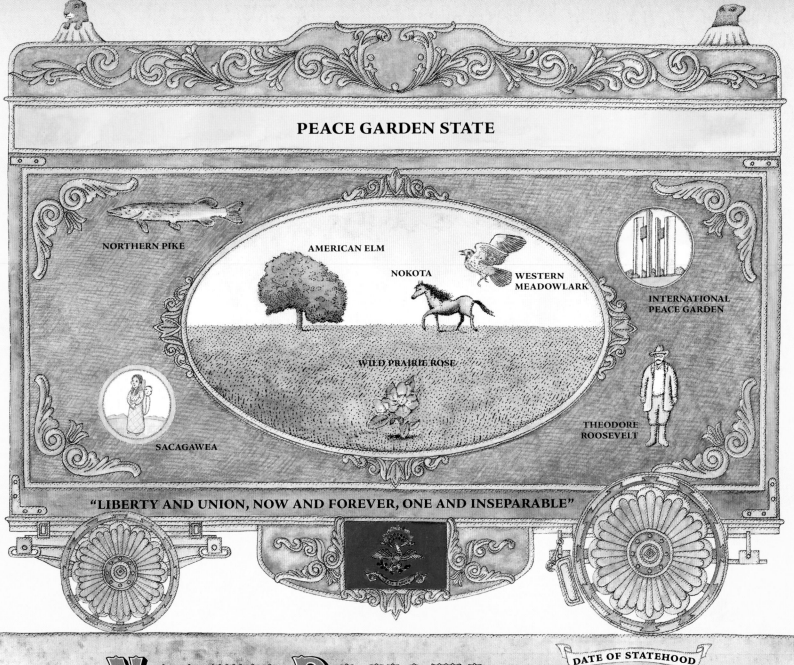

PEACE GARDEN STATE

NORTHERN PIKE

AMERICAN ELM

NOKOTA

WESTERN MEADOWLARK

INTERNATIONAL PEACE GARDEN

WILD PRAIRIE ROSE

SACAGAWEA

THEODORE ROOSEVELT

"LIBERTY AND UNION, NOW AND FOREVER, ONE AND INSEPARABLE"

39. NORTH DAKOTA November 2, 1889

DATE OF STATEHOOD

Named for the Sioux Indian word *dakota*, meaning "friend"

 Bismarck

 American elm

 wild prairie rose

western meadowlark

 North Dakota has 63 National Wildlife Refuges, more than any other state.

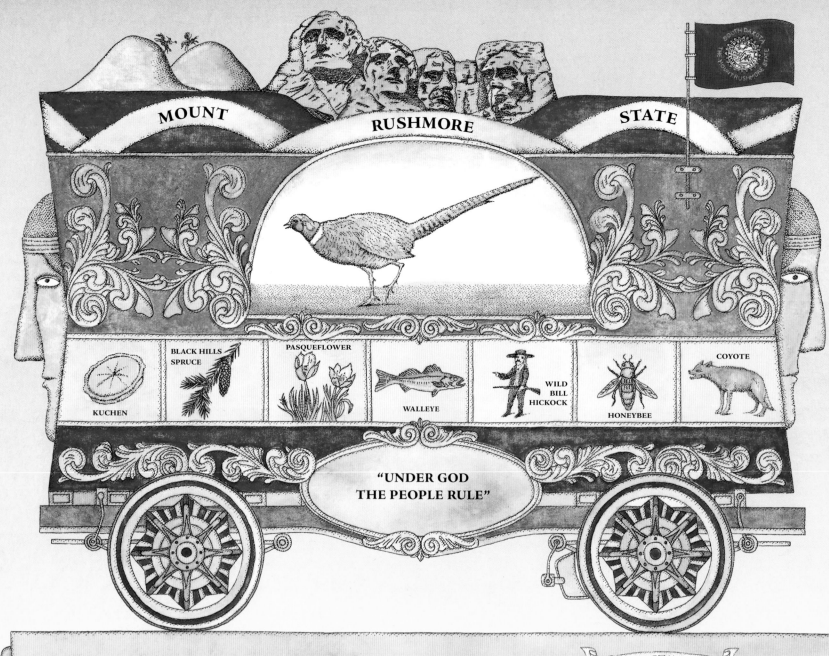

MOUNT RUSHMORE STATE

KUCHEN

BLACK HILLS SPRUCE

PASQUEFLOWER

WALLEYE

WILD BILL HICKOCK

HONEYBEE

COYOTE

"UNDER GOD
THE PEOPLE RULE"

DATE OF STATEHOOD

40. SOUTH DAKOTA November 2, 1889

Named for the Sioux Indian word *dakota*, meaning "friend"

 Pierre

Black Hills spruce

 pasqueflower

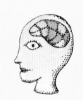 ring-necked pheasant

Sue, the largest and most intact *T. rex* fossil, was discovered by Sue Hendrickson in 1990 near the town of Faith.

BIG SKY COUNTRY

WESTERN MEADOWLARK

MOURNING CLOAK

TREASURE STATE

PONDEROSA PINE

MONTANA

BITTERROOT

"GOLD AND SILVER"

BLACKSPOTTED CUTTHROAT TROUT

DATE OF STATEHOOD

41. MONTANA November 8, 1889

Named for the Latin *montaanus*, meaning "mountainous"

 Helena

 Ponderosa pine

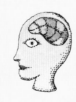 In Montana elk, deer, and antelope outnumber humans.

 bitterroot

 western meadowlark

STEELHEAD TROUT

EVERGREEN STATE

AMERICAN GOLDFINCH

APPLE

GREEN DARNER DRAGONFLY

PETRIFIED WOOD

"BY AND BY"

COAST RHODODENDRON

THE SEAL OF THE STATE OF WASHINGTON 1889

WESTERN HEMLOCK

DATE OF STATEHOOD

42. WASHINGTON November 11, 1889

Named for George Washington, the first U.S. president

 Olympia

 western hemlock

 Coast rhododendron

 American goldfinch

In 1980, Mount St. Helens, a volcano in the Cascade Range that had been dormant since 1857, erupted in one of the biggest volcanic disturbances in U.S. history.

GEM STATE

MONARCH

IDAHO STAR GARNET

SYRINGA

MOUNTAIN BLUEBIRD

WESTERN WHITE PINE

HUCKLEBERRY

CUTTHROAT TROUT

"LET IT BE PERPETUAL"

43. IDAHO July 3, 1890

DATE OF STATEHOOD

Name was coined or invented, and was originally used for a Columbia River steamship

 Boise

 western white pine

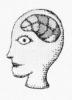 The state capitol building in Boise is heated by underground hot springs.

 syringa

mountain bluebird

OLD FAITHFUL

EQUALITY STATE

DEVILS TOWER

CUTTHROAT TROUT

WESTERN MEADOWLARK

INDIAN PAINTBRUSH

PLAINS COTTONWOOD

JADE

FIRST VOTE FOR WOMEN

"EQUAL RIGHTS"

44. WYOMING July 10, 1890

DATE OF STATEHOOD

Named for the Delaware Indian words meaning "at the big plains"

 Cheyenne

 plains cottonwood

 Indian paintbrush

 western meadowlark

Thousands of people traveling west on the Oregon Trail scratched their names on the surface of Independence Rock, which sits fifty miles southwest of Casper.

INDIAN RICE GRASS

BEEHIVE STATE

SEGO LILY

CALIFORNIA GULL

BLUE SPRUCE

BONNEVILLE CUTTHROAT TROUT

DUBHE

TOPAZ

CHERRY

ROCKY MOUNTAIN ELK

"INDUSTRY"

45. UTAH January 4, 1896

DATE OF STATEHOOD

Named for the Ute Indians (people of the mountains)

 Salt Lake City

blue spruce

 sego lily

California gull

Great Salt Lake is the fourth largest terminal (no outlet) lake in the world, three to five times saltier than the ocean, and free of fish (the largest marine creatures are brine shrimp).

SOONER STATE

BULL FROG

COLLARED LIZARD

BLACK SWALLOWTAIL

MISTLETOE

INDIAN BLANKET

FIDDLE

WHITE BASS

OKLAHOMA

REDBUD

SCISSOR-TAILED FLYCATCHER

"LABOR CONQUERS ALL THINGS"

46. OKLAHOMA November 16, 1907

Named for the Choctaw Indian words meaning "red people"

 Oklahoma City

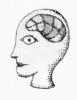 redbud

 mistletoe

 scissor-tailed flycatcher

 Oklahoma has the only state capitol building in the world with an oil well drilled beneath it.

LAND OF ENCHANTMENT

GEORGIA O'KEEFFE

TARANTULA HAWK WASP

BLACK BEAR

PIÑON

"IT GROWS AS IT GOES"

CUTTHROAT TROUT

YUCCA

47. NEW MEXICO January 6, 1912

Named by Spanish explorers, for Mexico

 Santa Fe

 piñon

 yucca

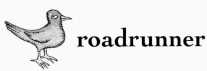 roadrunner

The city of Santa Fe was settled in 1607, making it the oldest state capital city in the country.

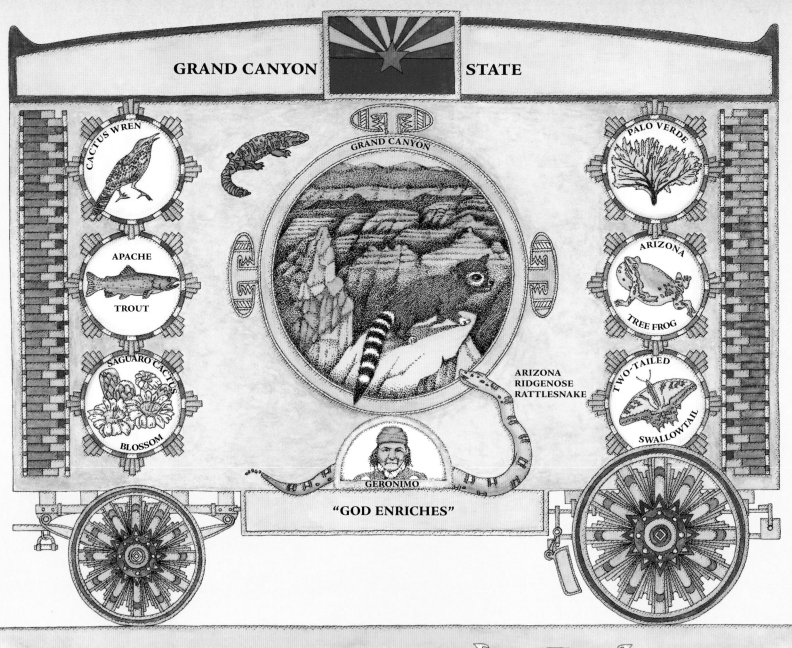

GRAND CANYON STATE

CACTUS WREN

APACHE TROUT

SAGUARO CACTUS BLOSSOM

GRAND CANYON

PALO VERDE

ARIZONA TREE FROG

TWO-TAILED SWALLOWTAIL

ARIZONA RIDGENOSE RATTLESNAKE

GERONIMO

"GOD ENRICHES"

DATE OF STATEHOOD

48. ARIZONA February 14, 1912

Named for the Papago Indian word *arizonac*, meaning "place of the small spring"

 Phoenix

 palo verde

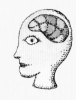 In 1930, Clyde Tombaugh at Lowell Observatory in Flagstaff discovered the planet Pluto.

 blossom of the saguaro cactus

 cactus wren

THE LAST FRONTIER

GOLD

FOUR-SPOT
SKIMMER
DRAGONFLY

MOOSE

BOWHEAD
WHALE

SITKA
SPRUCE

A WILLOW
PTARMIGAN

FORGET-ME-NOT

KING SALMON

"NORTH TO THE FUTURE"

DATE OF STATEHOOD

49. ALASKA January 3, 1959

Named for the Aleut word *alyeska*, meaning "great land"

 Juneau

 Sitka spruce

In Barrow, Alaska's northernmost point, the sun doesn't set for 84 days during the summer months.

 forget-me-not

 willow ptarmigan

NENE

KILAUEA

HALEAKALA

BLACK CORAL

QUEEN LILIUOKALANI

HUMPBACK WHALE

HAWAIIAN TRIGGERFISH

ALOHA STATE

YELLOW HIBISCUS

CANDLENUT

"THE LIFE OF THE LAND IS PERPETUATED IN RIGHTEOUSNESS"

DATE OF STATEHOOD

50. HAWAII August 21, 1959

Named for the Polynesian word *hawaiki*, meaning "homeland"

 Honolulu

candlenut

 yellow hibiscus

 nene

Honolulu's Iolani Palace is the only royal residence in the U.S.

"JUSTICE FOR ALL"

SCARLET OAK

WHITE HOUSE

WASHINGTON MONUMENT

WOOD THRUSH

CAPITOL

AMERICAN BEAUTY ROSE

LINCOLN MEMORIAL

WASHINGTON, D.C. July 16, 1790

Named in honor of George Washington and Christopher Columbus (District of Columbia)

 The capital of the U.S.

 American Beauty rose

scarlet oak

 wood thrush

 The Supreme Court has its own independent police force, which is responsible for a one-block area.

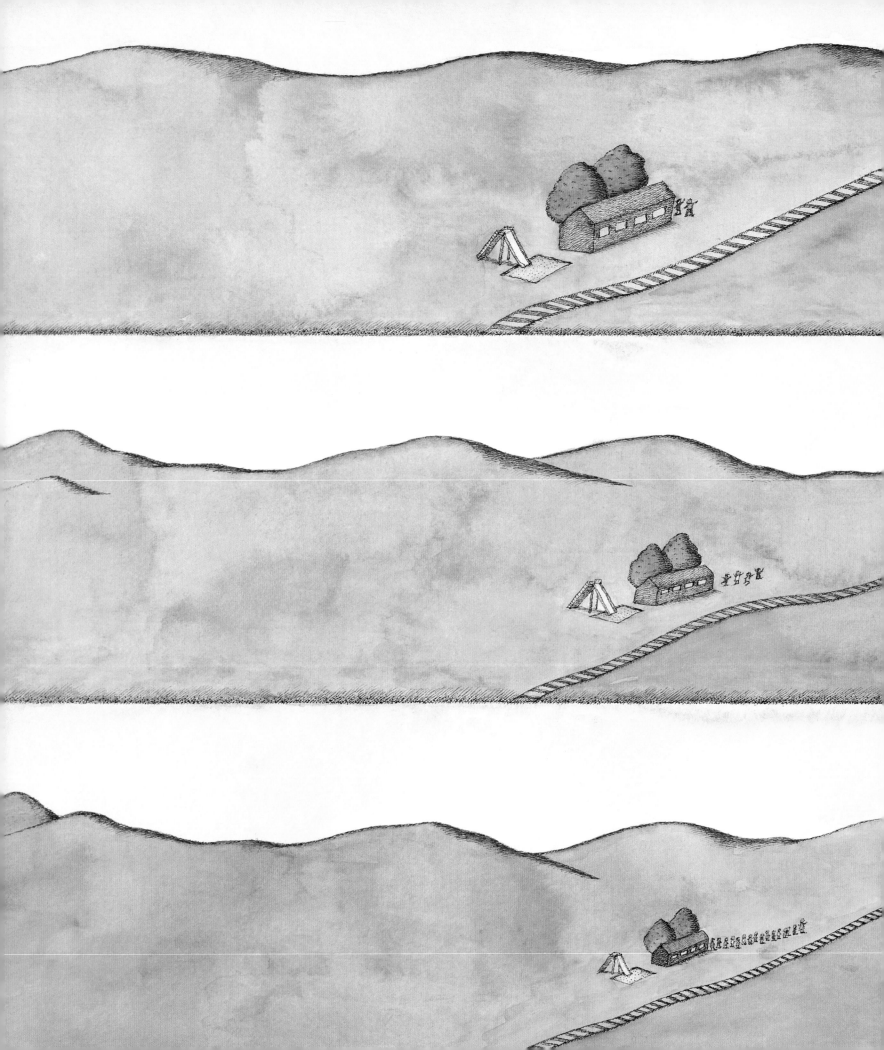

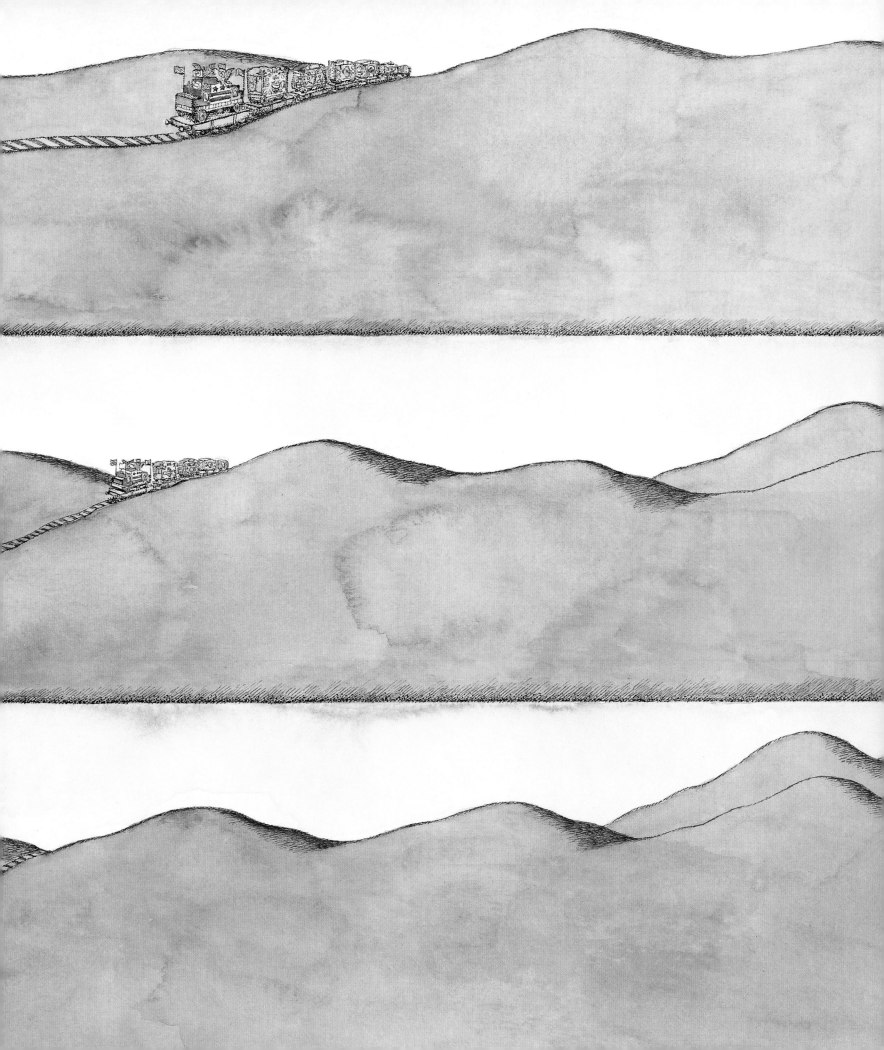